EMMANUEL JOSEPH

The Holy Entrepreneur, Merging Spiritual Growth and Business Skills for Kids

Copyright © 2025 by Emmanuel Joseph

All rights reserved. No part of this publication may be reproduced, stored or transmitted in any form or by any means, electronic, mechanical, photocopying, recording, scanning, or otherwise without written permission from the publisher. It is illegal to copy this book, post it to a website, or distribute it by any other means without permission.

First edition

This book was professionally typeset on Reedsy.
Find out more at reedsy.com

Contents

1	Chapter 1: The Seed of Greatness	1
2	Chapter 2: The Power of Vision	3
3	Chapter 3: The Value of Hard Work	5
4	Chapter 4: The Power of Prayer	6
5	Chapter 5: Building Strong Relationships	7
6	Chapter 6: The Importance of Honesty	8
7	Chapter 7: The Power of Generosity	9
8	Chapter 8: Embracing Creativity	10
9	Chapter 9: Learning from Failure	11
10	Chapter 10: The Power of Gratitude	12
11	Chapter 11: The Importance of Discipline	13
12	Chapter 12: The Power of Teamwork	14
13	Chapter 13: The Impact of Positive Attitude	15
14	Chapter 14: The Importance of Time Management	16
15	Chapter 15: The Joy of Giving Back	17
16	Chapter 16: The Power of Humility	18
17	Chapter 17: The Importance of Responsibility	19
18	Chapter 18: The Power of Communication	20
19	Chapter 19: Embracing Diversity	21
20	Chapter 20: The Role of Mentorship	22
21	Chapter 21: The Power of Adaptability	23
22	Chapter 22: The Importance of Listening	24
23	Chapter 23: The Power of Confidence	25
24	Chapter 24: The Joy of Learning	26
25	Chapter 25: The Legacy of the Holy Entrepreneur	27

1

Chapter 1: The Seed of Greatness

The journey of the Holy Entrepreneur begins with a simple seed. This seed isn't just any seed—it's the seed of greatness planted within every child. Just as a tree starts from a tiny seed, so does the potential for spiritual growth and business success in every young heart. Imagine a young boy named David, who lived in a small village. David loved stories about great leaders and was curious about how they became successful. One day, he met an old, wise gardener who taught him a valuable lesson.

The gardener gave David a small seed and asked him to plant it in his backyard. David was excited and followed the gardener's instructions carefully. He watered the seed every day, ensuring it got enough sunlight. Weeks passed, and nothing seemed to happen. David started to lose hope, but the gardener reminded him that patience and faith are essential. The seed needed time to grow roots before it could sprout.

As David continued to care for the seed, he also started to learn about patience, dedication, and faith. He realized that these qualities were not only important for growing plants but also for achieving success in life. The seed finally sprouted, and a small plant emerged. David was overjoyed and understood that greatness takes time and effort to develop.

The seed of greatness represents the potential within every child to grow spiritually and succeed in business. Just like David, kids need to nurture this seed with patience, dedication, and faith. The process may seem slow, but with consistent effort, their potential will eventually bloom. This chapter teaches kids that every small effort they make contributes to their growth, and they should never give up, even when progress seems slow.

The story of David and the seed serves as a powerful metaphor for the journey of the Holy Entrepreneur. By nurturing their inner potential with patience and faith, kids can achieve great things in both their spiritual lives and business endeavors. The seed of greatness is within every child, waiting to be nurtured and developed. With the right mindset and consistent effort, they can achieve their dreams and make a positive impact on the world.

2

Chapter 2: The Power of Vision

In a bustling town, there lived a girl named Sarah who had big dreams. Sarah loved painting and often imagined her artwork displayed in galleries worldwide. One day, while visiting the town's market, she met a kind artist who noticed her passion and encouraged her to keep pursuing her dreams. The artist taught Sarah that having a clear vision was the first step to achieving greatness.

Sarah's newfound mentor told her the story of Thomas, a young man who dreamed of creating a business that would help his community. Thomas had a vision of a store that would sell eco-friendly products, promoting a healthier environment. He drew a detailed plan of his store, complete with eco-friendly packaging and a section for educational workshops on sustainability. Thomas's vision was so clear that it inspired others to support his idea.

Sarah realized that just like Thomas, she needed to have a clear vision for her dreams. She began by creating a vision board, where she placed pictures and drawings of her goals. Every morning, Sarah would look at her vision board and feel motivated to take steps toward achieving her dreams. She also wrote down her goals in a journal, breaking them into smaller, manageable tasks.

Having a vision is like having a map that guides you toward your destination. It helps you stay focused and motivated, even when obstacles arise. Sarah learned that vision is not just about seeing the end result but also about believing in the journey. She started working on her paintings with renewed determination, knowing that each brushstroke brought her closer to her dream.

Sarah's story teaches kids the importance of having a clear vision for their goals. Whether it's a dream of starting a business or becoming an artist, having a vision helps them stay focused and motivated. By creating vision boards and setting clear goals, kids can turn their dreams into reality. The power of vision is a key element in the journey of the Holy Entrepreneur, guiding them toward success in both spiritual growth and business endeavors.

3

Chapter 3: The Value of Hard Work

Once there was a boy named Sam who dreamed of becoming a successful farmer. He was inspired by his grandfather, who had the most beautiful and bountiful farm in the village. Sam's grandfather taught him the value of hard work and dedication. Every day, Sam would wake up early to help his grandfather with various chores, from planting seeds to harvesting crops.

One day, a severe storm hit the village, and Sam's grandfather's farm was heavily damaged. Many of the crops were destroyed, and it seemed like all their hard work had been in vain. However, instead of giving up, Sam and his grandfather rolled up their sleeves and started rebuilding the farm. They worked tirelessly, replanting seeds and repairing the damage.

Through this experience, Sam learned that hard work and perseverance are essential for success. He realized that challenges and setbacks are a part of life, but they can be overcome with determination and effort. The farm eventually flourished again, and Sam felt a deep sense of pride in their achievements.

The value of hard work is a crucial lesson for young entrepreneurs. By putting in consistent effort and not giving up in the face of adversity, they can achieve their goals. This chapter teaches kids that success is not handed to them on a silver platter; it requires dedication, perseverance, and a strong work ethic.

4

Chapter 4: The Power of Prayer

Lily was a young girl who loved helping others. She often volunteered at her local community center, assisting with various activities and events. Lily's mother taught her the importance of prayer and how it could provide guidance and strength in times of need.

One day, the community center faced a financial crisis and was at risk of closing down. Lily felt devastated, as the center was a vital part of the community. She decided to pray for a solution, asking for wisdom and strength to help save the center. Inspired by her prayers, Lily came up with an idea to organize a fundraising event.

With the help of her friends and family, Lily planned a talent show to raise funds for the community center. They worked hard to promote the event, and on the day of the show, the turnout was incredible. The community came together, and the event raised enough money to keep the center open.

Lily's story teaches kids the power of prayer and faith. Prayer can provide guidance, strength, and inspiration in times of need. By combining prayer with action, kids can find solutions to their problems and make a positive impact on their communities. The power of prayer is an essential element in the journey of the Holy Entrepreneur.

5

Chapter 5: Building Strong Relationships

In a vibrant city, there lived a boy named Alex who had a natural talent for baking. He dreamed of opening his own bakery one day. However, Alex knew that to succeed, he needed the support of others. He started by building strong relationships with his family, friends, and neighbors.

Alex's mother taught him how to bake, and his father helped him with the business side of things. His friends supported him by spreading the word about his delicious treats, and his neighbors became his first customers. One day, Alex's bakery faced a challenge when a larger, well-established bakery opened nearby. Instead of feeling discouraged, Alex decided to focus on building even stronger relationships with his customers.

He organized community events, offered personalized services, and made an effort to get to know his customers better. His bakery became a beloved part of the community, and despite the competition, Alex's business thrived.

The story of Alex teaches kids the importance of building strong relationships in both their personal and professional lives. By fostering connections with others, they can create a support system that helps them achieve their goals. Building strong relationships is a key aspect of the journey of the Holy Entrepreneur.

6

Chapter 6: The Importance of Honesty

In a quiet village, there lived a girl named Emma who had a passion for storytelling. She loved writing and sharing her stories with others. One day, Emma heard about a writing competition and decided to enter. She worked hard on her story, pouring her heart and soul into it.

When the competition results were announced, Emma was devastated to find out that she didn't win. However, a few days later, she received a surprising letter from the competition organizers. They discovered that the winning story had been plagiarized, and they awarded Emma first place instead.

Emma's honesty and integrity earned her the respect and admiration of her peers and community. She learned that being truthful and honest is more important than winning at any cost. Her story teaches kids the importance of honesty in their spiritual and business lives.

Honesty builds trust and credibility, which are essential for success. By being truthful and maintaining integrity, kids can build a strong reputation and earn the respect of others. Honesty is a fundamental value for the Holy Entrepreneur.

7

Chapter 7: The Power of Generosity

In a small town, there lived a boy named Ben who loved helping others. He often noticed that some of his classmates didn't have enough school supplies or proper clothing. Ben decided to take action and organized a donation drive to collect items for those in need.

With the help of his family and friends, Ben set up collection boxes around the town and spread the word about the donation drive. The community responded generously, and soon, they had gathered enough supplies to help many students in need. Ben felt a deep sense of fulfillment knowing that his efforts made a difference in the lives of others.

The story of Ben teaches kids the power of generosity and how giving can positively impact their communities. By sharing their resources and helping those in need, kids can contribute to a better world. Generosity is a vital aspect of the journey of the Holy Entrepreneur.

8

Chapter 8: Embracing Creativity

Sophia was a girl with a vivid imagination and a love for art. She spent hours drawing, painting, and creating beautiful pieces of artwork. One day, her art teacher encouraged her to enter a local art contest. Sophia was excited but also nervous, as she had never participated in a competition before.

Determined to embrace her creativity, Sophia spent weeks working on her art piece. She experimented with different techniques and mediums, allowing her imagination to guide her. On the day of the contest, Sophia's artwork stood out, and she won first place. The experience boosted her confidence and inspired her to pursue her passion further.

Sophia's story teaches kids the importance of embracing their creativity and using it to express themselves. Creativity is not only essential for artistic pursuits but also for problem-solving and innovation in business. By nurturing their creative abilities, kids can develop unique solutions and stand out in their endeavors. Embracing creativity is a key element in the journey of the Holy Entrepreneur.

9

Chapter 9: Learning from Failure

Jacob was a boy with a passion for inventing. He loved creating gadgets and machines that could help people in their daily lives. One day, Jacob designed a device to make household chores easier. He was excited to show it to his family and friends, but when he tested it, the device didn't work as expected.

Feeling disappointed, Jacob considered giving up on his invention. However, his father encouraged him to see failure as an opportunity to learn and improve. Jacob took his father's advice and went back to the drawing board. He analyzed what went wrong and made adjustments to his design.

After several attempts and failures, Jacob's device finally worked perfectly. His persistence and willingness to learn from failure paid off. Jacob's story teaches kids that failure is not the end but a stepping stone to success. By learning from their mistakes and persevering, they can achieve their goals.

Failure is a natural part of the journey of the Holy Entrepreneur. Embracing failure and using it as a learning opportunity helps kids develop resilience and determination. This chapter emphasizes the importance of persistence and learning from setbacks.

10

Chapter 10: The Power of Gratitude

In a bustling city, there lived a girl named Mia who had a dream of becoming a chef. She loved cooking and experimenting with different recipes. Mia's parents supported her passion and encouraged her to pursue her dream. One day, Mia decided to organize a community dinner to showcase her culinary skills.

As Mia prepared for the event, she realized how fortunate she was to have supportive parents, access to fresh ingredients, and a community that believed in her. She felt a deep sense of gratitude and decided to express her appreciation through her cooking.

The community dinner was a huge success, and everyone enjoyed Mia's delicious dishes. At the end of the event, Mia thanked her parents, friends, and neighbors for their support. Her expression of gratitude created a positive and uplifting atmosphere, strengthening the bonds within the community.

Mia's story teaches kids the power of gratitude and how it can positively impact their lives and relationships. By appreciating the blessings and support they receive, kids can cultivate a positive mindset and build stronger connections with others. Gratitude is an essential aspect of the journey of the Holy Entrepreneur.

11

Chapter 11: The Importance of Discipline

In a quiet town, there lived a boy named Ethan who had a passion for playing the piano. He dreamed of becoming a renowned pianist and performing on grand stages. However, Ethan knew that achieving his dream required discipline and consistent practice.

Every day, Ethan set aside time to practice the piano, even when he felt tired or wanted to play with his friends. His piano teacher taught him that discipline was the key to mastering his craft. Ethan's hard work and dedication paid off when he was selected to perform at a prestigious music festival.

Ethan's story teaches kids the importance of discipline in achieving their goals. By developing a strong work ethic and staying committed to their pursuits, they can reach their full potential. Discipline is a crucial value for the Holy Entrepreneur, helping them stay focused and motivated on their journey.

12

Chapter 12: The Power of Teamwork

In a lively town, there lived a boy named Jack who loved playing soccer. His team had a big tournament coming up, and Jack was determined to win. However, he realized that individual talent alone wouldn't be enough to secure victory. Jack's coach taught the team the importance of teamwork and working together toward a common goal.

During practice sessions, the team learned to communicate effectively, support each other, and play to their strengths. They understood that each player had a unique role, and their combined efforts would lead to success. On the day of the tournament, Jack's team played with unity and coordination, ultimately winning the championship.

Jack's story teaches kids the importance of teamwork in achieving their goals. By collaborating and leveraging each other's strengths, they can accomplish great things. Teamwork is a vital aspect of the journey of the Holy Entrepreneur, helping them succeed in both spiritual and business endeavors.

13

Chapter 13: The Impact of Positive Attitude

In a quaint village, there lived a girl named Chloe who had a passion for gardening. She loved planting flowers and vegetables, bringing beauty and nourishment to her community. One day, a drought hit the village, causing many plants to wither and die. Despite the challenging circumstances, Chloe maintained a positive attitude and continued to care for her garden.

Chloe's optimism inspired her neighbors, and they joined her efforts to save the gardens. They collected rainwater, created shade structures, and used innovative techniques to conserve water. Slowly but surely, the gardens began to thrive again. Chloe's positive attitude not only helped save the plants but also brought the community closer together.

Chloe's story teaches kids the impact of a positive attitude in overcoming challenges. By staying optimistic and hopeful, they can inspire others and find creative solutions to problems. A positive attitude is an essential element in the journey of the Holy Entrepreneur, helping them navigate obstacles and achieve their goals.

14

Chapter 14: The Importance of Time Management

In a bustling city, there lived a boy named Ryan who had a dream of becoming a successful entrepreneur. He had many ideas and projects he wanted to pursue, but he often felt overwhelmed by the sheer volume of tasks. Ryan's mentor taught him the importance of time management and how to prioritize his responsibilities.

Ryan started by creating a schedule, breaking down his tasks into manageable chunks. He set specific goals for each day, ensuring he allocated time for work, rest, and leisure. With better time management, Ryan found himself more productive and less stressed. He was able to achieve his goals more efficiently and effectively.

Ryan's story teaches kids the importance of managing their time wisely. By setting priorities and creating a structured plan, they can achieve their goals without feeling overwhelmed. Time management is a crucial skill for the Holy Entrepreneur, helping them balance their spiritual growth and business pursuits.

15

Chapter 15: The Joy of Giving Back

In a close-knit community, there lived a girl named Olivia who loved baking. She often made delicious treats for her friends and family. One day, Olivia learned about a local shelter that provided food and support for those in need. She decided to use her baking skills to give back to her community.

Olivia organized a bake sale, with all the proceeds going to the shelter. She enlisted the help of her friends and family, and together, they baked a variety of treats. The bake sale was a huge success, raising enough money to support the shelter for several months. Olivia felt immense joy knowing that her efforts made a positive impact on the lives of others.

Olivia's story teaches kids the joy of giving back to their communities. By using their talents and resources to help others, they can make a meaningful difference in the world. Giving back is a fundamental value for the Holy Entrepreneur, fostering a sense of purpose and fulfillment in their journey.

16

Chapter 16: The Power of Humility

Once there was a boy named Liam who excelled in academics and sports. He often received praise and recognition, which made him proud. However, Liam's pride sometimes led him to overlook the contributions of others. One day, he participated in a group project and realized that his team members had valuable insights and skills.

Liam's teacher taught him the importance of humility and recognizing the strengths of others. Liam learned to listen and appreciate the contributions of his teammates. The project turned out to be a great success, and Liam understood that humility is a powerful quality that enhances collaboration and growth.

Humility is a crucial value for the Holy Entrepreneur. By acknowledging their own limitations and appreciating the strengths of others, kids can build stronger relationships and achieve greater success.

Chapter 17: The Importance of Responsibility

In a small village, there lived a girl named Zoe who loved taking care of animals. She dreamed of becoming a veterinarian and helping sick animals. One day, Zoe's neighbor asked her to take care of their pet dog while they were away. Zoe gladly accepted the responsibility.

Throughout the week, Zoe fed, walked, and cared for the dog diligently. She understood that being responsible meant taking her duties seriously and doing her best. When her neighbors returned, they were impressed with Zoe's dedication and trustworthiness.

Zoe's story teaches kids the importance of responsibility in their personal and professional lives. By taking their duties seriously and being reliable, they can earn the trust and respect of others. Responsibility is a fundamental value for the Holy Entrepreneur.

18

Chapter 18: The Power of Communication

In a bustling town, there lived a boy named Noah who loved public speaking. He enjoyed sharing his ideas and inspiring others. One day, Noah was chosen to represent his school in a regional speech competition. He knew that effective communication was key to making an impact.

Noah's speech coach taught him the importance of clarity, confidence, and connection with the audience. Noah practiced diligently, refining his speech and delivery. On the day of the competition, Noah's powerful and engaging speech earned him first place.

Noah's story teaches kids the power of communication in achieving their goals. By expressing their ideas clearly and confidently, they can inspire and influence others. Effective communication is an essential skill for the Holy Entrepreneur.

19

Chapter 19: Embracing Diversity

In a multicultural city, there lived a girl named Aisha who had friends from different backgrounds and cultures. Aisha loved learning about their traditions, languages, and stories. Her diverse friendships enriched her understanding of the world and broadened her perspective.

One day, Aisha's school organized an international fair where students could showcase their cultures. Aisha and her friends collaborated to create a vibrant and inclusive event, celebrating their diversity and promoting unity.

Aisha's story teaches kids the importance of embracing diversity and respecting different cultures. By appreciating and learning from diverse perspectives, they can foster inclusivity and harmony. Embracing diversity is a vital aspect of the journey of the Holy Entrepreneur.

20

Chapter 20: The Role of Mentorship

In a busy city, there lived a boy named Lucas who had a passion for science. He dreamed of becoming an inventor and creating innovative solutions to everyday problems. Lucas's neighbor, a retired engineer, noticed his interest and offered to mentor him.

Under his mentor's guidance, Lucas learned valuable skills and gained practical knowledge. His mentor's encouragement and support helped Lucas develop his ideas and bring them to life. Lucas realized the importance of having a mentor to guide and inspire him.

Lucas's story teaches kids the role of mentorship in their growth and development. By seeking guidance from experienced individuals, they can gain valuable insights and achieve their goals. Mentorship is a key element in the journey of the Holy Entrepreneur.

21

Chapter 21: The Power of Adaptability

In a dynamic town, there lived a girl named Ava who loved solving puzzles. She enjoyed the challenge of figuring out different solutions. One day, Ava's school introduced a new curriculum that required students to adapt to new teaching methods and technology.

Ava embraced the changes with a positive attitude and quickly adapted to the new environment. She realized that being flexible and open to change allowed her to thrive in different situations. Her adaptability helped her excel in her studies and become a role model for her peers.

Ava's story teaches kids the power of adaptability in navigating change. By being flexible and open to new experiences, they can overcome challenges and seize opportunities. Adaptability is an essential quality for the Holy Entrepreneur.

22

Chapter 22: The Importance of Listening

In a quiet village, there lived a boy named Oliver who had a talent for storytelling. He loved sharing stories with his friends and family. One day, Oliver's teacher taught him the importance of listening to others' stories and perspectives.

Oliver learned to listen attentively and empathetically, understanding the feelings and experiences of others. This newfound skill deepened his relationships and enriched his storytelling. Oliver realized that listening was just as important as speaking.

Oliver's story teaches kids the importance of listening in building meaningful connections. By being attentive and empathetic, they can understand and appreciate others' perspectives. Listening is a crucial skill for the Holy Entrepreneur.

23

Chapter 23: The Power of Confidence

In a vibrant city, there lived a girl named Emma who had a passion for dancing. She dreamed of performing on stage and inspiring others with her talent. However, Emma often felt nervous and doubted her abilities. Her dance instructor taught her the importance of confidence and self-belief.

Emma practiced diligently, focusing on building her confidence and honing her skills. Her instructor's encouragement helped her overcome her fears. On the day of the performance, Emma danced with grace and confidence, earning a standing ovation from the audience.

Emma's story teaches kids the power of confidence in achieving their dreams. By believing in themselves and their abilities, they can overcome challenges and shine. Confidence is an essential quality for the Holy Entrepreneur.

24

Chapter 24: The Joy of Learning

In a bustling town, there lived a boy named Max who had a curious mind. He loved exploring new subjects and discovering interesting facts. Max's parents encouraged his curiosity and provided him with books, puzzles, and educational games.

One day, Max's school organized a science fair where students could showcase their projects. Max eagerly participated, creating a fascinating display about the solar system. His project impressed the judges, and Max won first place.

Max's story teaches kids the joy of learning and the importance of staying curious. By exploring new subjects and seeking knowledge, they can develop a lifelong love for learning. The joy of learning is a fundamental value for the Holy Entrepreneur.

25

Chapter 25: The Legacy of the Holy Entrepreneur

In a flourishing town, there lived a girl named Mia who had learned valuable lessons throughout her journey. She combined her spiritual growth and business skills to create a positive impact on her community. Mia's journey inspired others to follow in her footsteps.

Mia realized that the true legacy of the Holy Entrepreneur is not just about personal success but also about making a difference in the lives of others. She mentored young entrepreneurs, shared her knowledge, and contributed to her community's growth and well-being.

Mia's story teaches kids the importance of leaving a positive legacy. By using their skills and values to help others, they can create a lasting impact on the world. The legacy of the Holy Entrepreneur is about inspiring future generations to pursue their dreams and make a difference.

Description

The Holy Entrepreneur: Merging Spiritual Growth and Business Skills for Kids

Embark on an inspiring journey with "The Holy Entrepreneur," a captivating book designed to ignite the entrepreneurial spirit in young minds while nurturing their spiritual growth. This book seamlessly blends valuable business skills with essential spiritual principles, offering kids a holistic approach to personal and professional development.

Through engaging stories and relatable characters, each chapter imparts timeless lessons that resonate with young readers. From the importance of hard work and the power of vision to the significance of humility and the joy of giving back, this book covers a wide range of topics that are crucial for success in life and business.

Young readers will follow the adventures of relatable characters like David, Sarah, and Mia as they navigate challenges, learn from failures, and celebrate their achievements. With practical advice and inspiring anecdotes, "The Holy Entrepreneur" empowers kids to dream big, work diligently, and make a positive impact on their communities.

This book is a must-read for parents, educators, and young aspiring entrepreneurs who seek to instill strong values and a growth mindset in the next generation. "The Holy Entrepreneur" is not just a guide to business success—it's a roadmap to a fulfilling and purpose-driven life.

Let this book be the guiding light for young minds as they embark on their own journey of merging spiritual growth and business skills, creating a brighter future for themselves and the world around them.

www.ingramcontent.com/pod-product-compliance
Lightning Source LLC
LaVergne TN
LVHW020741090526
838202LV00057BA/6157